experience
a fresh
explosion
of faith

*A taste of
Believing God*

"You are my witnesses," declares the Lord,
"and my servant whom I have chosen,
so that you may know and **believe me**
and understand that I am he"
(Isa. 43:10, author's emphasis).

Published by LifeWay Press®
© 2008 Beth Moore
Fifth printing 2012

ISBN 978-1-4158-6529-3
Item 005139183

Dewey decimal classification: 248.84
Subject heading: GOD \ CHRISTIAN LIFE \ FAITH

Unless otherwise indicated, Scripture quotations are from the Holy
Bible, New International Version, copyright © 1973, 1978, 1984 by
International Bible Society. Scripture quotations identified KJV are
from the King James Version. Scripture quotations marked HCSB®
are taken from the Holman Christian Standard Bible®, copyright
© 1999, 2000, 2002, 2003 by Holman Bible Publishers. Used by
permission. Scripture quotations identified as AMP are from the
Amplified Bible, © 1954, 1958, 1962, 1964, 1965, 1987 by
The Lockman Foundation.

To order additional copies of this resource, write to LifeWay
Church Resources Customer Service; One LifeWay Plaza;
Nashville, TN 37234-0013; e-mail orderentry@lifeway.com; fax
(615) 251-5933; phone toll free (800) 458-2772; order online at
www.lifeway.com; or visit the LifeWay Christian Store serving you.

Printed in the United States of America

Adult Publishing
LifeWay Church Resources
One LifeWay Plaza
Nashville, TN 37234-0152

table of contents

Introduction

A few years ago, while strengthening my grip on the Sword of the Spirit, God began wedging the Shield of Faith in my other hand so that I'd learn to use them the way He intended: in tandem. Mind you, I thought I had plenty of faith. After all, how much faith does a church-going, church-serving soul need? I would soon learn the answer: a whole lot more than I had. As forcefully as God has ever spoken to my heart, He said, "You believe in Me, Beth. Now I want you to believe Me."

Beloved, in His Word God made us promises. Real ones. Numerous ones that apply to our lives here on earth. Promises of things like all-surpassing power, productivity, peace, and joy. Few of us will argue the theory, but most of us don't live out the reality. I believe many of us, much like the children of Israel, wander in the wilderness of doubt with the promised land just on the other side of the river. This message has one primary goal: to encourage any Christian who will listen to move to his or her personalized place of divine promise and to flourish.

Many promises of God are unconditional, but His promises of full-throttle blessing, abundant life, fruit-bearing, and conquering are not. God has prepared more for you than your ears have heard, your eyes have seen, and your mind has ever conceived. The Creator of heaven and earth — the One with the entire universe and its riches at His disposal — knows you by name, has planned a promised land for you, and longs to bless you. He wisely reserves the right to require your cooperation.

Faith is the way believers jump on board with God and participate in countless wonderful things He has a mind to do. Faith happens when believers believe. My challenge to you, Dear One, is that you'll determine to grow in faith.

Throughout the next pages we'll take a closer look at the following five-step pledge of faith. I feel these statements can help us reclaim and live out our identities as heirs of the promise and children of God.

1. God is who He says He is.
2. God can do what He says He can do.
3. I am who God says I am.
4. I can do all things through Christ.
5. God's Word is alive and active in me.

This message is about developing an action-verb faith that invites the exhilaration of holy participation. Let's get out there where we can feel the wind of God's Spirit blowing in our faces! Let's determine to believe.

Chapter 1

God Is Who He Says He Is

The Lord is who and all that He claims. In fact, He's either everything He says He is or He's a liar and unworthy of any faith at all. Thankfully, Scripture tells us that no deceit can be found in Him.

Throughout Scripture, when God started moving in the lives of His people or instructing them to reposition, He began with a reminder: "I Am the Lord." Consider, for example, the case of the Israelites. God knew that the Israelites' certainty that the One who went before them was whom He claimed was their most powerful driving force in pressing toward their earthly destiny. That's why God constantly kept His identity and subsequent ability fresh in their minds.

- "I am the Lord, who brought you out of Ur of the Chaldeans to give you this land to take possession of it" (Gen. 15:7).

- "I am God Almighty; walk before me and be blameless. I will confirm my covenant between me and you and will greatly increase your numbers" (Gen. 17:1-2).

- "I am the God of your father, the God of Abraham, the God of Isaac and the God of Jacob. … I have indeed seen the misery of my people. … So I have come down to rescue them from the hand of the Egyptians and to bring them up out of that land into a good and spacious land" (Ex. 3:6-8).

- "God said to Moses, 'I AM WHO I AM. This is what you are to say to the Israelites: "I AM has sent me to you" ' " (Ex. 3:14).

o "Therefore, say to the Israelites: 'I am the LORD, and I will bring you out from under the yoke of the Egyptians. … And I will bring you to the land I swore with uplifted hand to give to Abraham, to Isaac and to Jacob. I will give it to you as a possession. I am the LORD' " (Ex. 6:6,8).

This concept is important to modern followers of God too. Psalm 100:3 carries a powerful punch easily missed in the poetry: "Know that the LORD is God." Know above all else that YHWH, our covenant Maker, is Elohiym, the God over all creation. In other words, you and I have got to know, not just hope or think, that the One who cut covenant with us through the torn flesh of Jesus

Christ is the same One who sits upon
the universe's throne, having spoken
the worlds into existence. Surrounded
by a society that spouts many gods but
at best nobly agrees to equate them, you
and I can *know* that the Lord is God.

Why is this important? Let's
consider Christ's questions to His
disciples. Christ prepared His small
band of followers to move into a land of
promise beginning "in Jerusalem, and in
all Judea and Samaria," then on to "the
ends of the earth" (Acts 1:8). In Caesaria
Philippi, Christ gathered His disciples
around Him and asked them two vital
questions that beg answers from us as
well. First, Christ asked, "Who do people
say the Son of Man is?" (Matt. 16:13).

Christ knew the potential power
of popular opinion. As we consider
that God is who He says He is, let's ask
ourselves who the people around us say

He is. In my life experience the most dangerously influential opinions are those held by intellectuals and scholars who profess Christianity but deny the veracity and present power of the Bible. To many the Godhead exists, but not exactly as Scripture says. Neither do they do (or still do) what Scripture says they can do. The obvious brilliance of these scholars supported by a convincing list of degrees tempts those who want to believe God's Word to feel gullible and ignorant. The unspoken indictment: "How could you be stupid enough to believe that?"

Sometimes the potential for humanly reasonable theologies to soothe and satisfy the follower's need to believe in *a* god leads to an acceptance of a lesser god not the God of Scripture. But Beloved, all human attempts to define God cannot help but minimize

Him. All attempts to take away the mystery and wonder that surround God leave Him something He is not. We cannot tame the Lion of Judah. A mystery, a wonder, and, yes, even a wildness about God exists that we cannot take from Him. Nor would we want to if we could grasp the adventure of Him. If we create a god we can fully explain, we concoct a different god from the Bible's. We must beware of recreating an image of God that makes us feel better. Of this fact I'm certain: If in our pursuit of greater knowledge God seems to have gotten smaller, we are deceived.

Who we believe God is greatly affects our eternal destinies, but I'd like to suggest that nothing has a greater effect on the quality of our lives and the fulfillment of our destinies on earth. Scripture bulges with evidence of God's power and greatness and His willingness to pour it into our lives. This is illustrated in the verses that follow Christ's paramount question to His disciples: "Who do you say I am?"

> "*Simon Peter answered, 'You are the Christ, the Son of the living God.' Jesus replied, 'Blessed are you, Simon son of Jonah, for this was not revealed to you by man, but by my Father in heaven. And I tell you that you are Peter, and on this rock I will build my church, and the gates of Hades will not overcome it. I will give you the keys of the kingdom of heaven; whatever you bind on earth will be bound in heaven, and whatever you loose on earth will be loosed in heaven'*" (Matt. 16:15-20).

Though Christ would build His church on the foundation of the apostles' testimonies, I don't think Peter understood Christ to say that He would build His entire church on His star pupil alone (compare 1 Cor. 3:11). In the Greek New Testament the word used for Peter is *Petros*, usually meaning "a stone, a piece or fragment" of a bigger boulder. The word used for the "rock" upon which Christ would build His church is *Petra*, usually meaning "a massive rock or cliff." Christ was pointing to Himself as the massive rock upon which He'd build His church and to Peter as the chip off the block whose testimony of Christ would pour the foundation for many. Peter was assigned tremendous position and responsibility in the kingdom when Christ said, "I will give you the keys of the kingdom of heaven" (Matt. 16:19).

In our paradigm, Peter received and would fulfill his earthly destiny first and foremost because he believed Christ was who God revealed Him to be. An undeniable link exists between believing God is who He says He is and fulfilling our God-ordained destinies.

As we consider God as whom He says He is, we're wise to ask ourselves the question: Who do I say God is? Many people and factors can influence who we've come to believe God is: our grandparents, our parents, our upbringings, our teachers, our friends, our enemies, our experiences, our health, our hardships, our counselors or therapists, and every conceivable form of media. If we attend church, our pastors and Bible teachers and their present or lacking authenticity undoubtedly shape our concept of God too. Have those factors led us to believe God is who He says He is? Someone less? Or someone simply different?

The beauty is that God is not changed one iota by who man says He is. Man's entire future, however, resides squarely upon its shoulders.

Beloved, God invites us to participate in kingdom affairs and yes, even kingdom authority under the rule of His righteous will. He extends staggering power to those willing to think with the mind of Christ rather than the mind of man. God will also empower His children to bind untold evils and strongholds if we'd believe Him and cooperate with Him. Where does this kind of existence begin? With biblical answers to the pivotal question, "Who do you say that I am?"

God is looking for stewards willing to bind their own unbelief in the mighty name of Jesus and loose a fresh anointing of faith. Are you ready?

CHAPTER 2

God Can Do What He Says He Can Do

Most biblical titles for God inseparably connect who He is to what He can do. For instance: as Savior, He saves; as Deliverer, He delivers; as Redeemer, He redeems; as Master, He assumes authority; as Bread of life, He provides; and as Almighty, He exerts divine strength. In short, God can do what He says He can precisely because He is who He says He is.

Before God insisted on calling me to fresh faith, I certainly believed He was who He said He was, but I was much less sure that He still works miracles. I was taught that God does not work many miracles today because we live in a different time period on the kingdom calendar. I think God had a fairly good time turning my neatly compartmentalized belief system upside down as He disproved that theory.

The issue at hand is the stronghold of unbelief in the church concerning biblical acts of God. For our purposes we'll call our two extremes cessationism and sensationalism. Simply put, cessationism teaches that more dramatic miracles no longer happen. Sensationalism teaches that the whole point of belief is miracles.

The former says God wants nothing to do with miracles now, and the latter depicts God as one big miracle machine. Christians tend to gravitate toward doctrinal extremes. So whose approach is correct on this issue? Scripture suggests neither is in the right.

In the Gospels Christ called those without faith to believe in miracles an "unbelieving and perverse generation" (Luke 9:41). On the other hand, He called those who focused entirely on miracles a "wicked and adulterous generation" (Matt. 16:4). If the modern body of Christ is set on cessationism or sensationalism, our choice is whether we'd rather be an unbelieving and perverse generation or a wicked and adulterous one. Both options share a commonality: Experience over faith is their underlying problem. Sensationalism seeks an experience, and cessationism believes only what it personally sees and experiences. Sensationalism suggests that everything possible is also probable, while cessationism accepts only the presently probable as the presently possible.

Either extreme is wildly offensive to God. Perhaps the most serious offense of sensationalism is its overwhelming tendency to be man-centered rather than God-centered, prioritizing what God can do over who He is. The reason Christ could dub miracle cravers as adulterous is because they worshiped God's wonders more than God Himself. Equally idolatrous, sensationalism suggests we can believe God as long as He does what we tell Him to do, as if we were the potter and God the clay.

WARNING TO HAVE PURE FAITH. JESUS IS ENOUGH!

Before you decide sensationalism is the worse offender of the two extremes, consider the wages of cessationalism. It not only cheats the believer of the pleasure and coinciding rewards of God that come to those who exercise faith (Heb. 11:6); it also severely undercuts hope.

Beloved, the God we serve is able (Dan. 3:17). Everything is possible (Mark 9:23). Nothing is impossible (Luke 1:37). We can always hope and pray diligently for a miracle.

If, in God's sovereignty, He chooses to accomplish His purposes another way, let it not be that we have not because we asked not (Jas. 4:2) or that we have not because we believed not (Matt. 9:29).

Second Corinthians 1:20 tells us that "no matter how many promises God has made, they are 'Yes' in Christ." Christ gave His life so God could say yes to the fulfillment of His promises in the lives of believing mortals. Therefore, I am utterly convinced that anything an earnestly seeking child of God receives from the throne is for the sake of a greater yes, whether realized on earth or in heaven. A present-active-participle believer will see miracles, all right. Sometimes the greater miracle may be abundant life, redemption, ministry, and exceeding harvest after a "no" we felt we wouldn't survive. If you dare to believe and you don't get your miracle, God has a greater one planned. Stay tuned. If what you desperately need or deeply desire is founded in the Word of God, don't let anyone tell you that God

can't … or that He undoubtedly won't.
Beloved, God is "Wonderful" (Isa. 9:6). In
fact, remove the wonders from God, and
you can no longer call Him wonderful.
The wonder factor of God still exists!

I believe a host of reasons explain
why the present body of Christ witnesses
fewer miracles and wonders than the
early church, but for our purposes I
wish to highlight two. The first one is a
personal conviction that is surely obvious.
I fear we are a dreadfully unbelieving
generation, particularly the portion of
us in the prosperous West. Reports of
miracles come out of many Third World
countries where all they seem to have
is faith. More locally, however, we are
caught in a tragic cycle. We believe little
because we see little, so we see little
and continue to believe little. It's time
we dumped this wobbling cycle for a
form of transportation that really gets us

somewhere. In order to make the trade-in, we must cease to accept the visible as the possible and start believing what God says over what man sees.

The second reason we see fewer miracles may reflect an ounce of what some cessationists weigh by the ton. Though I know wonders haven't ceased because I've seen and experienced them, I won't argue that according to His sovereignty, God may have greater purpose and higher priorities for more widespread miracles in some generations and geographies than others. My argument is that we could use some profound works of God in our here and now, and He may just be waiting for us to muster up some corporate belief and start asking Him. Even many cessationists believe that a day of miracles and wonders will come again before the end of times. My questions are simple: Why can't that be now? Must it wait? Could God even now be waiting for a revival of faith? He is the Initiator, the very Author, of faith (Heb. 12:2). Could this restlessness and dissatisfaction we feel in our souls be Christ initiating and authorizing a new day of awakened faith and outpoured Spirit? Oh, God, let it be.

Please don't misunderstand that believing God only involves believing Him for dramatic miracles. If we don't include believing Him for the miraculous, however, can you imagine the tragedy of all we could miss?

Certainly ours is not the first generation missing widespread wonders. Gideon's generation, way back in Old Testament days, found itself under terrible enemy oppression. They hid in strongholds and fell into an ineffectiveness far removed from their promised position. Impoverished,

Initiate in me, O Lord, write out a story of faith on my heart.

the Israelites cried out to the Lord for help. Check out what happened next: "When the angel of the LORD appeared to Gideon, he said, 'The LORD is with you, mighty warrior.' 'But sir,' Gideon replied, 'if the LORD is with us, why has all this happened to us? Where are all his wonders that our fathers told us about?'" (Judg. 6:12-13).

Psalm 74 intimates that when God withheld wonders, His thinking people assumed something was wrong (as did Gideon), and the wise rightly searched for the disconnection. Verses 9 and 11 say, "We are given no miraculous signs; no prophets are left, and none of us knows how long this will be. ...Why do you hold back your hand, your right hand?" Verse 22 pleads, "Rise up, O God, and defend your cause."

If in reality we see few wonders of God in the midst of His people and through His people, shouldn't we as well inquire why? Are we not equally desperate? Is God no longer willing to intervene miraculously and wondrously in our behalf? We are surrounded by a dying and depraved world, mounting violence and the threat of mass destruction, disease, plague, enticing false religion, and a surging fury of satanic assault and seduction. We are desperate for the wonders and miracles of God. We need Him to show His mighty arm and tell the world that He is alive, active, and very much with us.

Oh, that the church would fall on its face and cry out the words the prophet Habakkuk cried: "LORD, I have heard of your fame; I stand in awe of your deeds, O LORD. Renew them in our day, in our time make them known" (3:2).

Believe that God can, Beloved. He is still in the miracle business.

CHAPTER 3

I Am Who God Says I Am

Believing I am who God says I am necessitates choosing what God says over what I feel. This proves more difficult than any other faith challenge I face. For the most part, my deep insecurity and uncertainty are based on a messy conglomeration of early childhood victimization and a long-term history of defeat. But I want so much to live as a woman of faith. In fact, I'd give just about anything to be a woman God could characterize by her faith since nothing pleases Him more (Heb. 11:6).

If I'm really serious about believing God, I have to believe God about me. But as I consider the challenge, I wonder about all those historical figures

listed in the Hebrews 11 hall of faith.
Do you think some of them had a little
trouble believing they were who God
said they were? I can't answer for all of
them, but Moses certainly did. The first
question he asked God after hearing
His voice from the burning bush was,
"Who am I, that I should go to Pharaoh
and bring the Israelites out of Egypt?"
(Ex. 3:11). Later in the conversation
Moses had the ire-raising audacity to
respond to his call, "O Lord, please send
someone else to do it" (Ex. 4:13).

Moses had his own reasons for
resisting his call and his new identity
as God's servant, but we share at least
one. He too had terrible sin in his past. I
wonder about Joshua, though. Scripture
paints him as a mighty warrior and
a true worshiper who tarried in the
presence of God. We read no history of
failure. At first we might assume he was

confident and ready for anything, but immediately following God's official command for his life, the first chapter of Joshua could intimate something to the contrary.

Repetitions are usually telling in the Bible, and within a few short verses God told Joshua to "be strong and courageous" no less than three times. The second time He preceded the word "courageous" with a descriptive "very." Now why would God repeat a call to courage to a stalwart, confident, and fearless hearer? I'd like to suggest God's man of the hour was quaking in his sandals.

Numbers 13 records a rarely publicized fact about Joshua that I find compelling. At the time of the first exploration of Canaan, he is listed in the census of leaders as "Hoshea son of Nun" (v. 8). A parenthetical portion of verse

16 informs us that at some unspecified point "Moses gave Hoshea son of Nun the name Joshua." Scripture is clear that Moses knew Joshua would lead the conquest (Num. 27:18-20). We may not know when Joshua received his new name, but we don't have to be biblical scholars to reason why he might have needed one. In essence, the name Hoshea means "deliverer" while Joshua (Jehoshua) means "Jehovah delivers." If I were chosen by God to lead a grasshopper people into a land of giant opposition, I'd want to know He, not me, was the true Deliverer. I'd like to suggest that Joshua not only needed to know who he was but he also needed to know who he wasn't. He wasn't God; neither are we.

So, who does God say we are? Who are you in Him? If we've received Jesus as our personal Savior, the sum of our identity is found in First John 3:1:

"How great is the love the Father has lavished on us, that we should be called the children of God! And that is what we are!" Beloved, God spent no small amount of inspired ink expressing the various facets of sonship and daughtership. Perhaps the most concentrated assessment of who we are in New Testament Scripture is found in Ephesians 1:3-8 (HCSB):

> "Blessed be the God and Father of our Lord Jesus Christ, who has blessed us with every spiritual blessing in the heavens, in Christ; for He chose us in Him, before the foundation of the world, to be holy and blameless in His sight. In love He predestined us to be adopted through Jesus Christ for Himself, according to His favor and will, to the praise of His glorious grace that He favored us with in the Beloved. In Him we have redemption through His

blood, the forgiveness of our trespasses,
according to the riches of His grace that
He lavished on us with all wisdom and
understanding."

If we knew nothing else the New
Testament says about us but accepted
these few truths into our belief system,
our lives would be forever altered. We
are blessed, chosen, adopted, favored,
redeemed, and forgiven.

Beloved, believing we are who
God says we are has enormous results.
Consider just a few: A dramatically
strengthened sense of security.
Chosen, adopted, favored. What more
could we need in order to feel secure?
I love the phrase the King James
Version uses instead of "favored." We
are "accepted in the beloved." If our
stubborn minds absorb that we are
accepted by God because Jesus Christ,

our choices and subsequent behaviors
are profoundly affected.

Understand that while it isn't always
easy to believe we are who God says we
are, blessing comes to those who do!
Romans 4 frames one of my favorite
revelations in all of Scripture: "Abraham
believed God, and it was credited to
him as righteousness. Now when a man
works, his wages are not credited to him
as a gift, but as an obligation. However,
to the man who does not work but trusts
God who justifies the wicked, his faith is
credited as righteousness."

Beloved, absorb this principle:
Every time we believe God, He credits
it to our account as righteousness. The
most obvious assumption is that God
credits righteous acts as righteousness,
but the prophet Isaiah penned the
disclaimer: "All of our righteous acts are
like filthy rags" (Isa. 64:6). God insists in

Scripture that believing Him is what He credits to our account as righteousness, and He gets to make the rules. As if to answer the skeptics who would try to deny the application to believers through the centuries, God removed all doubt in Romans 4:23,25: "The words 'it was credited to him' were written not for Moses alone, but also for us to whom God will credit righteousness—for us who believe in him who raised Jesus our Lord from the dead."

I'd like to make a final observation on believing we are who God says we are in the context of Romans 4. Not coincidentally, this chapter of Scripture framing the concept of faith credited as righteousness specifies two Old Testament figures as examples: Abraham and King David. They lived in very different eras and fulfilled different positions, yet they shared

one commonality that related heavily
to the concept of faith credited as
righteousness. Both men sinned
so grievously that their faith was
demanded to believe they were still
who God said they were: a father of
multitudes and a king whose kingdom
would never end.

True restoration demands faith.
The apostle Peter could certainly attest
to that, too. Jesus said, "Simon, Simon,
Satan has asked to sift you as wheat. But
I have prayed for you, Simon, that your
faith may not fail. And when you have
turned back, strengthen your brothers"
(Luke 22:31-32).

Why did Christ pray specifically for
Simon Peter's faith not to fail? Peter's
future was not dependent on a perfect
track record. It was dependent on his
faith. Peter would desperately need
the courage to believe he was still who

Christ said he was even after publicly denying Him. The result? The old fisher of men did indeed turn back and strengthen his brothers.

Peter believed God, and it was credited to him as righteousness. Sometimes the hardest biblical truths to accept are about us. Believe you are who God says you are and fathom the double blessing of God crediting it to you as righteousness.

CHAPTER 4

I Can Do All Things Through Christ

Philippians 4:13 claims that a servant of God can do all things — all things — through Christ who gives him strength. That includes the otherwise impossible. God will give you every place you step your feet for the glory of His name if you'll only let Him.

I loved broadening our scope to include Joshua, Abraham, and David in the last chapter. Each of their names made the team cut in the Hebrews 11 hall of faith. I was surprised and somehow refreshed to think that a measure of their challenge to walk by faith was likely found in continuing to believe what God said about them in spite of fears and failures. Isn't it encouraging to realize we're not alone in our struggles?

I'd like to now set our sights back on Joshua, our primary protagonist, because he specialized in leading God's children to their promised lands of faith and fruitfulness. Joshua had a reputation for believing God against all odds. Though he lived centuries before Jesus, his example offers endless applications to New Testament believers. Joshua's life helps us understand and accept our fourth statement of faith: I can do all things through Christ. Through the might of the living God, Joshua did what he knew he could not do. Like us, he was told in advance he'd be able. We might call it preassurance rather than reassurance.

Let's take a fresh look at that preassurance in Joshua 1:1-9:

"After the death of Moses ... the Lord said to Joshua son of Nun, Moses' aide: 'Moses my servant is dead. Now then, you and all these people, get ready to cross the Jordan River into the land I am about to give to them — to the Israelites. I will give you every place where you set your foot, as I promised Moses. Your territory will extend from the desert to Lebanon, and from the great river, the Euphrates — all the Hittite country — to the Great Sea on the west. No one will be able to stand up against you all the days of your life. As I was with Moses, so I will be with you; I will never leave you nor forsake you. Be strong and courageous, because you will lead these people to inherit the land I swore to their fore-fathers to give them. Be strong and very courageous. Be careful to obey all the law my servant Moses gave you; ... that you may be successful wherever you go. Do not let this Book of the Law depart from your mouth; meditate on it day and night, so that *you may be careful to do everything written in it. Then you will be prosperous and successful. Have I not commanded you? Be strong and courageous. Do not be terrified; do not be discouraged, for the LORD your God will be with you wherever you go.'"*

Down through the ages in the Old Testament, God seemed to speak and accomplish much of His work through one primary individual (or at the most a few). Abraham, Isaac, Jacob, Joseph, Moses, Joshua, David, and an arm-long list of prophets pose a few examples. By and large, God chose to accomplish His agenda most often through simple math: One plus one.

I'd like to suggest that John the Baptist may have been the last prophet in the One plus one equation. As "a voice of one … in the desert" he cried, "Prepare the way for the Lord" (Matt. 3:3). Beloved, the fullness of the Godhead Himself came down from heaven to forever fulfill the one man calling to all humanity. Jesus "the One and Only" came from the Father, full of grace and truth" (John 1:14).

No matter how mighty servants like Moses and Joshua were, "one and only" shoes tend to run large and slap around awkwardly on a walk. When Christ came to earth, He stepped His feet into those shoes, and for the first time in all of history, they were a perfect fit. From that moment on God's plan was not to use just one but many: a corporate body of believers for each generation, each bringing his or her gifts to the mix.

Christ broke the mold from the very beginning when He purposely commissioned 12 apostles. Christ called the Twelve to join Him in the work He was doing. He commissioned them and supernaturally empowered them to accomplish divine tasks in His name. Further, Luke 10:1 tells us that "after this the Lord appointed seventy-two others and sent them two by two ahead of him to every town and place where he was about to go." They too were equipped and empowered to do in His name what they otherwise couldn't. Bug-eyed to be sure, they did "all things through Christ" who gave them strength (Phil. 4:13, KJV).

New Testament math didn't stop with 12 plus 72. In the Gospel of John, Christ gave the open invitation and basic requirement for accomplishing remarkable works in His name: "I tell you the truth, anyone who has faith in me will do what I have been doing. He will do even greater things than these, because I am going to the Father" (John 14:12). Anyone. That's a wide-open roster.

Christ's final instructions before leaving earth were, "Go and make disciples of all nations, baptizing them in the name of the Father and of the Son and of the Holy Spirit, and teaching them to obey everything I have commanded you. And surely I am with you always, to the very end of the age" (Matt. 28:19-20). Let's get over the mentality that God mightily uses a few chosen people in each generation to fulfill His kingdom agenda and everyone else is basically insignificant. You were meant to bring forth much fruit. You can be effective. Powerfully used. I'm talking to you. Not your preacher or Bible study teacher. Your legacy can still have an impact in a dozen generations if Christ tarries. You don't have to look a certain way, receive a certain gift, attend a certain denominational church, practice a certain kind of ministry, or establish a nonprofit organization! All you need to be mighty in your generation is a shield of faith and the sword of the Spirit (the Word of God, Eph. 6:16-17). Through Christ you can absolutely, unequivocally do anything God places before you (Phil. 4:13).

So why do we so often balk at the task? I believe the answers lay in Joshua 1. There God warned Joshua not to fall for two of the most effective deterrents to a promised-land existence. "Do not be terrified; do not be discouraged." In our previous chapter we touched on the element of fear in our mention of insecurity. I'd like to explore it further at this time because fear is the very factor that keeps many of us from fleshing out our fourth statement of faith. We can do all things through Christ who strengthens us, but frankly we won't if we're too afraid or too discouraged to try.

Remember, where need abounds, grace more abounds. God's mercy is new every morning, and like manna in the wilderness, He apportions it according to our need. If you struggle with fear or feel bound up with discouragement, God offers hope!

Understand that Joshua never faced anything so frightful or potentially disparaging that God didn't see him through it. As if to remind him of the facts, God said, "The LORD your God will be with you wherever you go" (Josh. 1:9). When Jesus told His disciples not to be afraid in the storm, the reason wasn't the removal of their frightful circumstances but the presence of their Savior. "Take courage! It is I. Don't be afraid" (Matt. 14:27).

Remember, faith is never the denial of reality but is a belief in a greater reality. In other words, the truth may be that terrifying or terribly discouraging circumstances surround you. The reason you don't have to buckle to fear and

discouragement is the presence of God
in the middle of your circumstances.
Call upon Him to step His One and
Only shoes onto your territory and take
over like the commander of the Lord's
army (Josh. 5:15). Hear Him say to you
the words He said to Joshua: "Take off
your sandals, for the place where you
are standing is holy." That place, that
circumstance, is holy because God stands
on it with you. You don't have to fill His
shoes, Dear One. Take off your sandals and
walk barefoot in His wake.

Beloved, whether or not you want
to admit it, God gifted you out of His
glorious grace and for His name's sake.
Christ has spoken over your life as His
present-day disciple: "This is to my
Father's glory, that you bear much fruit,
showing yourselves to be my disciples"
(John 15:8). Perhaps, like me, you have
grievously failed God in the past. Perhaps,

like me, your prior confidence was unknowingly in your own ability and determination to stay on track. I honestly thought my genuine love for the Lord would keep my handicapped feet on the path all by itself. I clearly remember telling God that no one would ever love Him more than I and that He'd never be sorry He called me. Then I fell headfirst into a pit. Tragically, not for the last time. Over and over the words rung in my head like church bells drowning in discord: I failed God! I failed God!

Somehow I don't think I'm the only one who ever felt that way. Failure takes all sorts of forms and hits all sorts of unsuspecting, sincere followers of Jesus Christ. We don't have to sin grievously to feel like we've failed. Sometimes all it takes is feeling like we've proved ineffective and untalented too many times to try again. What about you? Do you feel like you've failed God in some way? Are you too scared or discouraged to try serving God again? Do you allow Satan to demoralize you by preying on your fear that you are nothing more than a failure? Then hear these words: God–will–not–fail–you!

Grab onto the Lord with everything you have. Cast yourself entirely on His ability to succeed and not yours. Blind yourself to all ambition except to please Him. Walk in His shadow. Grab onto the hem of His garment and find the healing and grace to go where He leads. In that place you will be equipped to do the impossible. There you can do all things through Christ who strengthens you.

Dear One, let Christ intercede for you according to the will of His Father. He knows the plans He has for you. Plans to give you a hope and a future. You can because He can.

CHAPTER 5

God's Word Is Alive and Active in Me

An ongoing relationship with God through His Word is essential to the Christian's consistent victory! Making the study of God's Word a priority is undoubtedly the best place to start.

Beloved, we can't presently and actively believe God in our day-to-day challenges if we are not presently and actively in His Word. Romans 10:17 offers the most obvious link: "So then faith cometh by hearing, and hearing by the word of God" (KJV). God's direction for our lives will escape us without the Word of God as "a lamp unto our feet and a light unto our path" (Ps. 119:105).

Further, liberty in Christ becomes a reality in life through knowing and applying the truth of God's Word, not just taking our Bibles to church or keeping them on our nightstands. Psalm 119:11 implies that hiding the Word in our hearts is a major safeguard against sin. Ignoring God's Word is inexcusable if we honestly seek to live for Him.

Ephesians 6:17 states that God's Word is our Sword of the Spirit, but we have to learn how to use it if we want to be a powerful force for the kingdom and against the darkness. God set the standard with Joshua when He told him to keep the Word continually on his tongue, to meditate on it day and night, and to live by its commands. "Then you will be prosperous and successful" (Josh. 1:8). With all my heart I believe living on and by God's Word is still the key to true success.

I seem to have a new favorite verse every day, but Hebrews 4:12 (AMP) is high on the list:

> "For the Word that God speaks is alive and full of power [making it active, operative, energizing, and effective]; it is sharper than any two-edged sword, penetrating to the dividing line of the breath of life (soul) and [the immortal] spirit, and of joints and marrow [of the deepest parts of our nature], exposing and sifting and analyzing and judging the very thoughts and purposes of the heart."

Don't miss the crucial tie between the Word of God and the people of God in this verse. God not only told us that His Word is alive, effective, and powerful on its own — He insisted that it is alive, effective, and powerful in us when we receive it. Pause and let that truth sink in. I'm convinced most of us don't begin to appreciate and assimilate this revolutionary precept. Unlike any other text, the Word of God has supernatural effects for those who receive it by faith. When we receive it by reading it, meditating on it, believing it, and applying it, the life of the Word becomes lively in us. The power of God's Word becomes powerful in us. The activity of the Word becomes active in us. The operations of the Word become operative in us. The energy of the Word becomes energizing in us. The effectiveness of the Word becomes effective in us. In fact, according to Hebrews 4:12, when we receive God's Word, it invades every part of our being, even the marrow of our bones and the motives of our hearts.

God doesn't speak just to hear the sound of His own voice. Interestingly, neither does He speak to be heard by others. He speaks to accomplish. This aim proves consistent from the beginning of time. Genesis 1:3 records the first words out of His mouth where humankind is concerned: "And God said, 'Let there be light,' and there was light." Isaiah 55:10-11 expresses the intention of His Word:

> "As the rain and the snow come down from heaven, and do not return to it without watering the earth and making it bud and flourish, so that it yields seed for the sower and bread for the eater, so is my word that goes out from my mouth: It will not return to me empty, but will accomplish what I desire and achieve the purpose for which I sent it."

God's Word possesses accomplishing power and achieving power. That's a fact.

But I want it to have accomplishing and achieving power in me. That's why I'm very intentional about thanking the Lord for the quickening power of His Word in me, claiming and believing that He is energizing it to accomplish and achieve His desires. I welcome and receive its power in my life.

As I sit before God on my back porch every morning and place that day's schedule and petitions before Him in prayer, I receive my daily Bible reading like an athlete might eat an energy bar. I often read that day's portion of the Word aloud and actively participate in receiving it into my belief system. (I do this by taking a moment to meditate on it. I might ask myself questions such as: "Do I really believe these words? And, if I do, how does it show? How might I be able to act on the truth of these words today? How do these words apply to my present challenges and petitions today?" I also ask God to take those words and sow them deep into my otherwise deceptive heart and even into my subconscious mind.) I count on those Scriptures in my morning Bible reading to become active, energizing, and powerful in me that day. And they do.

Beloved, if your expectation of God's Word in your life has been small, I am asking you to consider giving it far more credit. Second Timothy 3:16 says, "All Scripture is God breathed," so don't just read it like any other inspirational or instructional text. Inhale it!

Jeremiah 15:16 says, "Your words came, I ate them; they were my joy and my heart's delight, for I bear your name, O Lord God Almighty." Try Jeremiah's approach while you're at it. Don't just read God's Words. Receive them like a famished man at a feast. Whether we imagine inhaling it or devouring it, "let the word of Christ dwell in [us] richly" (Col. 3:16). Ask God to cause it to abide in you and bring its properties of effervescent life, power, and effectiveness with it. How about something moving into your life with some positive baggage for a change? Believe God to accomplish and achieve something eternal and intentional through your daily Scripture meditation. Grow in confidence that every word abiding in you has powerful effects.

When we receive Christ as Savior, the actual Spirit of Christ, the Holy Spirit takes up residence in us. God's Word has such an effect on a believer's daily life due to its vital association with the Holy Spirit. First Corinthians 6:19 refers to us as temples of the Holy Spirit.

The Holy Spirit has a strong connection to the Word of God. John 14:17 calls the Holy Spirit the "Spirit of truth," and 2 Timothy 2:15 calls Scripture the "word of truth." In the same way that sin quenches the Holy Spirit within us, Scripture quickens the Holy Spirit within us. When we are filled with the Holy Spirit by yielding to His lordship and we read and receive God's Word, something virtually supernatural takes place. You might think of it as internal combustion.

Let me explain. In Jeremiah 23:29 God said, "Is not my word like fire?" As we draw from this parallel, relating something we can't quite understand to something we can, picture the Holy Spirit like a flammable substance within us. Because oil was often associated with anointing in the Word, many scholars believe oil symbolized the Holy Spirit. For the sake of our analogy, imagine the Holy Spirit as flammable oil within us. Now imagine this oil flooding us completely as we seek and receive by faith the filling

of God's Holy Spirit. Next imagine taking
the torch of God's Word and combining
it with the oil of the Holy Spirit. What is
the result? The consuming fire of our God
blazes within us, bringing supernatural
energy, glorious activity, and pure,
unadulterated power. If you like formulas,
this is one I believe you can count on:
Sometimes I actually feel the Holy Spirit
within me quickening to the Word of God
as I study it, mix it with faith, and pray to
absorb it. Even when I don't feel a thing, I
count on supernatural fireworks within.

God says His Word is alive and
powerful, and I believe Him. He also says
His Word is alive and powerful when it's
in me. Me: a bundle of faults, fears, and
insecurities. Just think! My weakness is
not strong enough to wound God's Word.
Neither is yours. God does His job. He
speaks to accomplish. We don't have to
make Him. We just need to let Him.

Conclusion

As I've mentioned throughout this booklet, Hebrews 11 is commonly called the hall of faith. There God lovingly recorded a testimony of flesh-and-blood faithfulness. If you'll glance at it, you'll see that the segments follow an inspired pattern:

By faith ... Abel ... (v. 4)
By faith ... Enoch ... (v. 5)
By faith ... Noah ... (v. 7)
By faith ... Abraham ... (v. 8)

By faith ... Isaac ... (v. 20)
By faith ... Jacob ... (v. 21)
By faith ... Joseph ... (v. 22)
By faith ... Moses ... (v. 23)
By faith ... Rahab ... (v. 31)

Each passage recounts the story of a man or woman so enamored with God that belief in Him overshadowed all else. Hebrews `11:40 fittingly concludes the chapter with a reference to us — to all believers who would follow in the footsteps of faith. I want to be in that hall of faith, Beloved. In fact, my heart's desire is that you'll believe God for every promise intended for the soil of earth and persevere faithfully until the full inheritance of heaven too.

Our destiny as believers is not to live in fear and defeat but to live in victory. The only way we'll ever meet our earthly potential as Christ's followers is to start believing God on every plane, from agreeing with who He says He is to trusting that He cares about our everyday needs.

Beloved, as we go our separate ways, may we commission one another to spend our lives devouring God's Word. We have only one certain way of knowing that

God is who He says He is.

God can do what He says He can do.

I am who God says I am.

I can do all things through Christ.

The way we can know these truths is expressed in our fifth statement: God's Word is alive and active in us. Breathe it. Believe it. Speak it. Live it. Love it. And brace yourself for a wild ride that will last a lifetime.

About the Author

Beth Moore has written best-selling Bible studies on the tabernacle, Psalms of Ascent, David, Paul, and Jesus. Her books *Breaking Free*, *Praying God's Word*, and *When Godly People Do Ungodly Things* have all focused on the battle Satan is waging against Christians. *Believing God* and *Living Beyond Yourself* focus on how Christians can live triumphantly in today's world. Beth has a passion for Christ, a passion for Bible study, and a passion to see Christians living the lives Christ intended.

Beth is an active member of First Baptist Church of Houston, Texas. The wife of Keith, mother of young adult daughters Amanda and Melissa, and grandmother to Jackson, Beth serves a worldwide audience through Living Proof Ministry. Her conference ministry, writing, and videos reach millions of people every year.